Roots

by Sandy Stream
Illustrated by Yoko Matsuoka

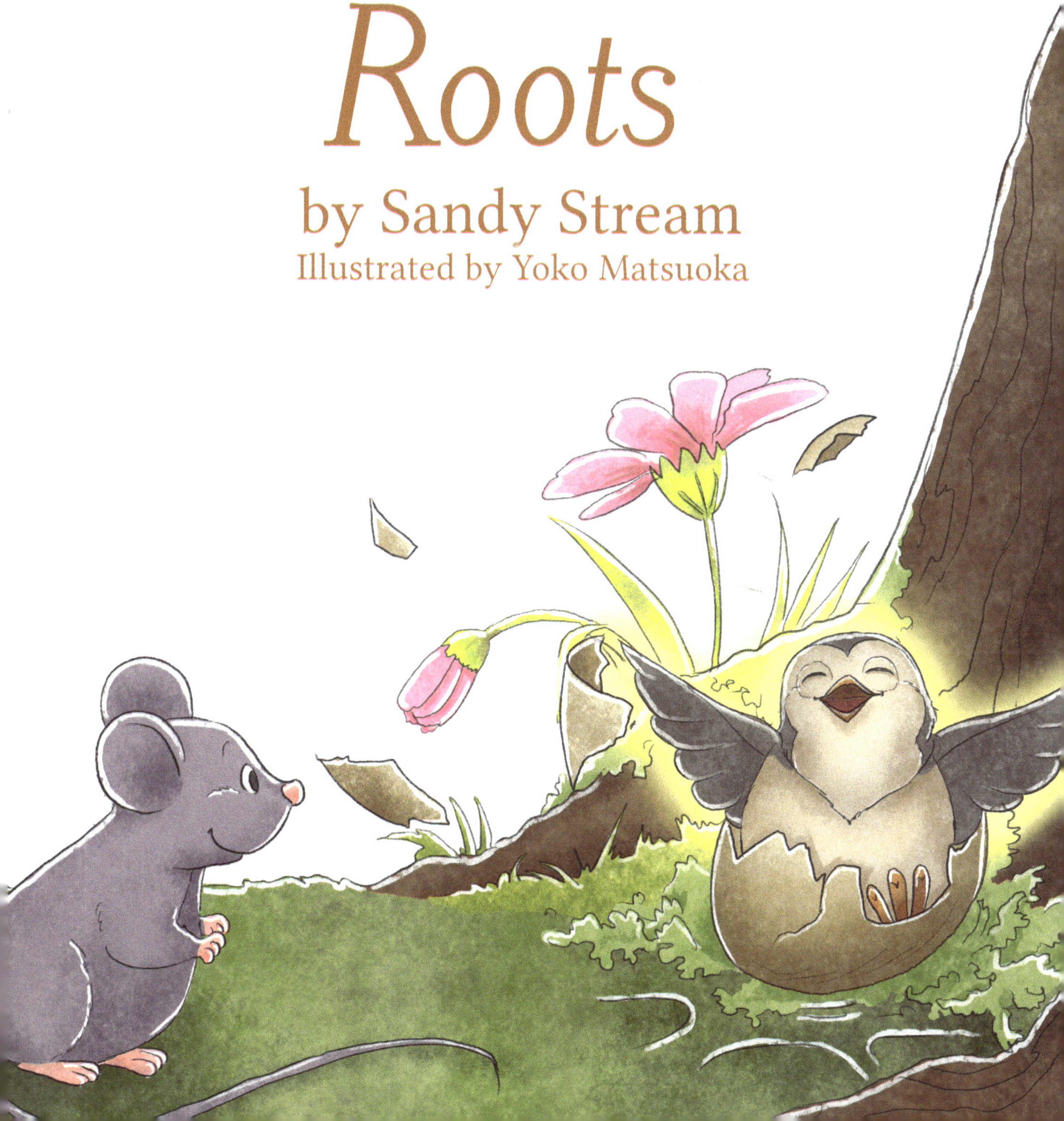

Roots. By Sandy Stream
Illustrated by Yoko Matsuoka
Edited by Tomoko Matsuoka

ISBN 978-0-9739481-6-5

Copyright © 2014 by Sandy Stream Publishing. Montreal, Canada.
All rights reserved. No part of this book may be reproduced, stored in a retrieval system, or transmitted in any form or by any means without the written permission of Sandy Stream Publishing.

On a Personal Note

I have met many people like Roots in my life. You can recognize them easily from the look in their shining eyes, which can transform almost anything that happens to cross their paths.

There are moments where my own eyes can see what Roots sees, but it is not consistent. I am still learning from those individuals who seem to shine.

I know that it is possible for each of us to see clearly like Roots can.

Sandy Stream

Based on a *few* true stories

Once upon a time, there was a great wind that shook an owl's nest. One of the eggs fell out and landed on the soft moss near a great oak tree.

When the owl was born, his heart was filled with happiness, joy, and sunshine. The little animals of the forest called him "Roots" because he was born near the roots of the great oak.

Roots got up and started to walk...

He loved to walk and feel the warm earth underneath him.

He loved to eat berries from the nearby bushes and all kinds of seeds.

One day, as Roots was walking along, a white rabbit hopped in front of him and froze in fright.

The owl sensed that the rabbit was afraid and said, "Please do not be afraid. I will not eat you."

"Why not?" asked the white rabbit, perplexed.
"Because you are alive," answered the owl.
"And I don't want to change that."

Rabbit and Roots became friends and walked around the world together...

One spring day, as they walked along, they arrived at a part of the world where many birds with tornadoes and hurricanes stuck inside were fighting each other.
"Why are the birds fighting?" the rabbit asked.
"They cannot see what is happening inside themselves," the owl said sadly. "It is too difficult for them to see the truth."

In the fall, they arrived at a part of the world where many birds with holes in their hearts and tweets stuck in their throats were busy and lost.

"Why are the birds so busy?" Rabbit asked Roots.

"Because they don't want to see. Keeping busy allows them to avoid looking at their pain. So they prefer to be blind."

In the winter, they arrived at a part of the world where many birds with armor looked very serious and guarded.

"Why do the birds look so unfriendly?" Rabbit asked.

"Because they have locked themselves up to protect themselves. They cannot see anything anymore."

"Let's go to the mountain!" said the little white rabbit.

Rabbit skipped playfully along as Owl walked up the mountain. When they reached the top, they sat quietly and breathed the fresh air.

"Let's go to the river!" said the little white rabbit.

When Rabbit and Roots arrived at the river's edge, they sat and listened to the water and tasted its purity.

Many seasons passed, and Roots got older. One day, Rabbit went to the river to cry. He knew that he might lose his friend in a short time. At the river, he saw Beaver.
"What's wrong?" Beaver asked.
Rabbit explained how he felt.
"I'm sorry, Rabbit," said Beaver. "The wise blind owl is very special indeed."
Blind? wondered Rabbit.

Rabbit went back to Roots. "What is it like not being able to see?" Rabbit asked.
Owl smiled and said, "I don't know, my dear friend… Ask the birds you saw on our travels."
And then he smiled:
"Dear Rabbit, it is only when our eyes are closed that we can actually see the truth."

And with those words, the owl closed his eyes. He observed the whole world inside and outside himself, and then peacefully joined the earth...

...and on that very spot grew a beautiful tree.

The always

The River Series

Sparky Can Fly
Sparky's Mama
Tweets and Hurricanes
Feathers
Flex
Roots
The River

www.RiverSpeaks.com

www.ingramcontent.com/pod-product-compliance
Lightning Source LLC
Chambersburg PA
CBHW061121010526
44112CB00024B/2941